HOMEMADE
MUD PIES

Also by Annie:

Words of a Magpie

Also by Aaron:

Novels:

Stars Below the Concrete
Battles (Book II in the Stars Series)
August Likes My Hue

Poetry Collections:

Cracked Green Door
Things I Never Knew

Comics:

Grey (writer)

HOMEMADE
MUD PIES

ANNIE THOMPSON
-AND-
AARON QUINN

WALNUT STREET
—PUBLISHING—

it all started with an onion

...AND I CATCH THE ENORMITY

Dead retina riddles
was I depressed in my mother's womb
or is enormity engorging mundanity
to force an autopsy of my brittled attempt at normalcy-
all my friends float in lava lamps.
Skip dead-speak for boulder word enormity,
leaving poetry in the street like a no trespassing sign
Running, walking dancing but I do not cross the line.
Facing myself is harder than filling the void with shapes and
sounds that echo off the pavement - dead things, not living things.
All my friends float by in the ultraviolet fog.
Can a cauldron of moths glow in my fear?
                    I do not float,
I sink to the zigzagged bottom of the swamp-
this is the womb of hidden trauma-
all my friends have skulls to pick and bricks to shatter windows.
I don't dare ask them to shatter mine- don't pull me out -
I sit at the bottom of the empty mine-
Bartering with my own mind
To feed me just a tablespoon of normalcy
until I am ready to be consumed by enormity

NOT BEFORE YOU TASTE MY GRUDGE ON TOP OF LOOKOUT MOUNTAIN, WHERE THE GHOSTS SIT AND WAIT FOR ANOTHER ROMANCE TO DRINK

Cracked open - I want to crawl back into my shell
Pistachios and oysters empathize
Put me back inside
Out here - I'm being swallowed whole

      my skin holds me like a grudge
               where did the mud under my nails
come from?
      my skin holds me like a grudge

splice me open from birth to faith

Finding my faith again is like
Digging for clams in the marsh
Do I bury myself or unbury God
I was taught rest is a sin - my skin holds me together

Like a grudge

      let me

feel
    the
          void
concrete gospels devour my faith,
      dissolve my hope and give me doubt
my skin holds me like a grudge - this too will decay.

HAVE YOU EVER HELD A FRAGMENTED dream
WHILE WAITING FOR THE SCHOOL BUS?

a survival guide to the soft-hearted:
gather clay from cracked wastelands and
water it down with tears
slather it on your skin until it hardens
in the heat of rising tempers.

find the frothing silence of night and listen to the abandoned day
still the moment in visions of mad, rad big bangs that explode
real as the flood that breaks through
examine the pattern of self on the wall-

fragments on the ground are still fragments of you.

AT THE FEET OF TIME- ELEPHANTS VIEW US AS CATS AND JUST WANT US TO BE HAPPY, SASSY, AND UNASHAMED

I am often surprised when the jagged edges of the world
Do not catch on the fabric of my soul
Tearing open whatever softness is there
Pouring out all that is inside –
                    a river of rainbows and blood.

dead angels do not sing but they bleed in the
streets until the saints weep-

            the wings are clipped

            my wings are clipped

When did it happen? The feathers pulled and broken
Over many moments of my memory
Laying in an iridescent kaleidoscope pile
At the feet of Time.

Do not put the ashes on my forehead,
Spread them on my tongue,
time cannot be burned to ashes,

it is not like me when standing knee deep
in the winter creek

Wondering, wondering –
will I disintegrate into dust if I stand still long enough?
Or will the cold water wake my bones
And wash the
            imaginary blood from my hands

A cleansing-

    cleansing

        cleansing

the creek is my blood of the lamb
        be still my soul,
        the angels wings are clipped, too.

MUSHROOM SERMONS AND WIDE-EYED STARES AT THE WATERFALL THAT KICKED A SNAKE OFF THE MOUNTAIN

Are there red ants in the wild pink roses?
Is there an ant on each five petals?

drop bits of time on the holy altar at the stems
the otherness of stillness blooms with grace

baritone sermons are not the gospel-
the bee landing on the yellow center is shalom:

am I as the ant?
Is this chaos I live within
only a flower blooming briefly?

Prayers from the lips of ladybugs
    find me in the nameless temple
searching for the lord of the ants.

OUR CONFESSIONS ARE LONGER THAN THE DISTANCE TO MARS CAUSE BABY, LIFE IS NOT FUN WITHOUT ENOUGH MISTAKES TO BUILD SANDCASTLES THAT COLLAPSE DURING HIGH TIDE

Claw marks and cobwebs crowd the inside of my head.
How will paper birds fly when their wings
get swept up in these storms?
I try to water myself like a potted Pansy in hopes the fog will clear
But the bucket dried up–
                    you can't use what you already gave away.

I feel plastic, as though I am cracked down the side
like my soul is a perpetual earthquake:
Can a plastic hand create art?
Create something out of nothing
like a vengeful god looking to flood a sinking ship!
If my destiny is to be broken, then shatter me.

My curse (my gift) is to build crystal cities out of the fragments.
Flood the open road with streams of devoured dreams,
i will mud-stuck run until freedom splices into orange-slice.
breakfasts- a lassoed rock will not turn into a bullfight
but a fragmented curse will fit symmetrically in my plastic hand-
I'll sit inside this glass palace and clear the cobwebs
Fill the buckets with water from these dream streams and scream:
"My soul is an earthquake, but now it will crack the worldwide
instead of making my hands shake"

my plastic hands are tired, not deterred.

8

HOLD IT, HOLD IT LIKE A BAD DREAM ON A SATURDAY NIGHT

stomachs full of yacketyakking after kicking in jaws
and line sculpting eye sockets
to understand the world with an edge.

            the windowpanes remain intact-
we have failed at rebelling against
the urge to go into air-conditioned.
mind traps, baby the mouse sure
don't know the cheese will kill it-
ain't that some fate gift wrapped in social mores.

the monster under the bed only
grows as big as the cage we build inside our heads.
one match is enough to burn bones to dust.
but instead, we let bodies of lost art keep piling up
every poem we stifle to make room for industrialized poison
            is a murder-
                  resurrect them all
and maybe their flood will crack the glass.

flick the oxidized tip, burn the pipes inside our veins.
come waltz with our murder, come waltz with decorum.
or leave your footsteps on the drain grates on main street.
waltz with our murder and throw fertilizer in our hands
when the graves get too full and
hums of passion emit from the ground.

soil-dark confetti won't keep them buried,

you will not keep us buried,
clawing at the throat of the sacrilegious dancing on tombstones.
the path of the creative is littered
with barbed vines and barbed wire -
veins full of the dead words of the uninspired .

tell me the carnival is town,
tell me the snail shell is empty
tell me the rusted pennies
          on my tongue will lug me to the junkyard
tell me when the tomb cries out for the poems left in my womb
or just waltz with me when there is another murder
crickety crawling down the sidewalk.

          this is my mouse parade

BACK AND FORTH, BACK AND FORTH, SOMETIMES AND I AM AND OTHER TIMES I AM NOT, WILL YOU WAIT FOR ME TO DECIDE?

i, a pendulum
Consumed by vining emotions
Or scorching the earth, freezing them out.

Swing.

    Swing.
        Swing.

The frost covered my windshield
a painted match lights a nearly waxless candle.

Swing.

Like a bad dream revving for a new cycle every midnight
    i am five with sticky hands,
    i am eighteen eviscerated by the world

    Swing.

i hope the dynamics of my soul still clash inside me
When my hands wrinkle like winter leaves
When i was three i flew from a

       Swing

And before the ground crunched
the air from my lungs, I was free.

PEELED FLESH ISN'T ALL BAD IF IT REPRESENTS AN EPIC CHANGE FROM BEING A DISASTER TO AN ACTUAL DISGRACE

The doors to this circus have opened
Enter at your own risk or throw your talent in the ring
My best act is trying to balance
While walking across all my torn and tangled strings.

Crack my spine open to pour in the bleach,
Consume me,
Consume me,
Consume me like I only have worth
if your acidic eyes are peeling off my flesh
Tie my wishful tongue with stripped thorns,
the carousel goes around and around
Until... has it ever stopped?
The shadows ride the circle whispering an ember song-

The show is for you... for who?
Strings attached to straining joints,
pull...pull...pull me until I break apart
Puppet shows always made me
think about the universe and the invisible strings
How much originality do any of us really think?

the universe is in me. does it bleed?
does it rip its tongue out and hand it to the sun?

I am abstract
I am vapor
Abstract vapor
lacks originality

but seeps into the pores of the carousel
      as my bleached spine u bends until
my ripped-out tongue tastes the sun.

Taste it like the fire eaters
Like the fire ants that dance in a parade around my head
Venom swims in a hundred stingers just beneath my skin
But I tear out my own fangs while the onlookers make me bleed.

I am consumed with their gravel stares
I am consumed while their bleached shoes step over my spine.

The carousel goes

            around
                  and around
                        and around.

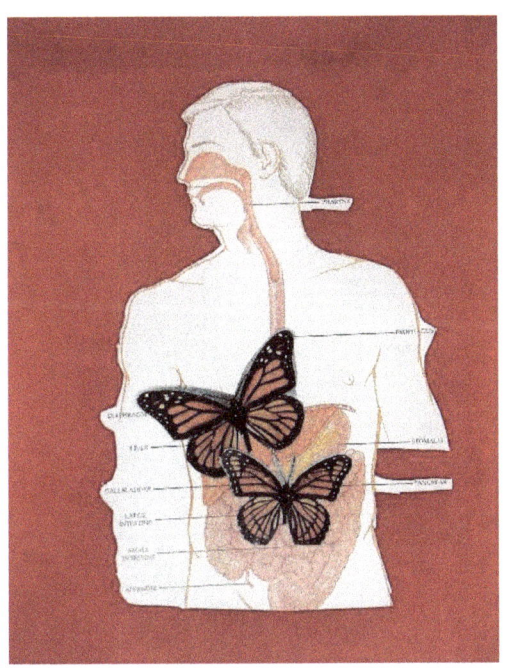

THIS TIME, MAYBE THERE IS NOT A THIS TIME, MAYBE THERE IS ONLY A COLLECTION OF REVEBRATING LAST TIMES

or i will perish while wandering up the tree in my eye
or i will snap the rubber band
and watch the world flip on its head
or i will sit with your lavender sunrise,
dissecting my knuckles until the candle goes out

to find the crow who perches on the branches of my mind
to break the binding that holds reality upright
to lay with chartreuse-bladed grass healing
my hands until the moon sets

when i only miss pollinated light that dissipates behind
claustrophobic relationships
when i only sledgehammer my words onto naturally dyed paper
when I only smell cherry blossom blooms in the spring

15

so i crawl into a bed of flowering brambles to wrap myself in a
cocoon of thorned armor
so, my resurrected feelings will bring sleeping fibers to life and
grow a forest
so the ghost of flowers will follow me into the darkest days of
winter

there is no resurrection without a soldered shut casket where the
worms join the disco
there is no darkest days unless i deny the light three times then a
fourth for posterity
there is no healing unless i drink the nails that i found bloodied
in the dirt

and dancing along, my soul will begin to beat
and be washed in kaleidoscope color
and in the dark, it will grow roots that no longer slumber
and the nails that fell from heaven's hands will build our bones
instead of breaking them

this is my ...
        faith/doubt
this is my ...
        love/regret
this is my ...
        hope/honesty

        whose reflection should i use as a mirror, now?

SORRY, SO SORRY, THE NIGHT CAME QUICKER THAN I EXPECTED NOW I FEEL LIKE THERE ARE SOME WINDOWS TO SMASH

My organs work in orchestra,
chasing breath that escapes into the night.
When light dissipates and I am left in droplets with my thoughts
veils hang heavy like dragonfly wings.
You can see through them
but the world looks shattered on the other side.

A shared icon is not a shared belief-
        diaphanous hope,
        the dull fat of aguey faith dropped in the dew.

And thus tiny pieces of my soul

have floated away like flower seeds
in the winds of the world - washed away in the rains.
I do not miss them –
I think perhaps they landed in people and places
and grew gardens
of Dandelions

The gas mask is on tonight.
The blocks trundle by,
Like stepping into a perfectly placid pool:
Give up the shimmering,
breathable air for depths you've never known
without words gorging my lips:

the silence is eternal.

Then there is a field with dead petal perfume.
Then there is a room with live limbs
avoiding the strings and eating jasmine rice.
Then there is my childhood street
where the shadows still stalk like rain during the flood-

the strings sing to me. the street is a marionette lullaby,
pulling my legs to dance,
dance puppet, dance,
or become our serpentarium.

I have no umbrella for the rain.

JUST BECAUSE I HAVE A NAME DOES NOT MEAN I HAVE AN IDENTITY, BLEED MY NAME INTO A BELL JAR THEN I CAN FINALLY BE SOMETHING WITH WEIGHT

Call me Calypso
I search for the things I've lost in catacombs
Hidden gems sparkling beneath stone tombs
I cannot remember them all.

Memory hangs from a small wire
swinging back and forth:
A pedagogy of things lost and things found.

Where is the fountain with the disturbed water?
Where my maimed jawbone can be reset
to speak what I have forgotten?

Drip
        Drip
                Drip

Goes drops of the blood of my heart
Into the depths
Each time what was lost returns
And bites into me.

I leave the hallway frames hanging sideways,
wires be damned,
                        skewed, matching my tilted head gai.t

A world on its side fits just right as the memories

D
   r
      i
        p

Stalactites reach down.
Are they offering me something to cling to?
Or are they teeth coming to drink me?
Eyes watch me from the frames, waiting for me to remember.

Lick the flames off my unrepentant tongue.
I devour other's eyes like morphine,
wondering if i am blind
when my self-worth is found in what i swallow.
Lick the flames off my tongue, make me holy when i hear the

Drip
Drip
Drip

No matter how deep in the sea I am bound,
the fire burns, the monster churns
raking at my ribs from within
searching for what I have forgotten
      for the faded ink in the polaroid,
      for the hymns lost near January frozen lakes.

With each remembered, my scars

    Drip

Drip

      Drip

ITALY OR CHATTANOOGA BOTH HAVE ROADS THAT CAN LEAD TO A DARKNESS THAT ENGULFS OUR SHADOWS AND ILLUMINATES THE STREET LIGHTS

Will they lose me to Italy?
Lose me to a path in a vine-blocked forest?
     Staying has felt vulgar,
     a curse that agitates the morning

My mind breaks.

Will you find me in the back streets of small towns?

Find me on a walk somewhere I've never been before.
I long to wander like a cloud buffeted in promising winds.
Faded words on wrinkled paper weave my mind back together.

Summer suns lost inside the time-stained beams of the barn-
        country Narnia found in damp plywood
        and rotting cabinets,
apophatic imagination in a maelstrom blender of gentle days:
have they already lost me?

so, i howl.

A sound laced with lost things and found
heirlooms in forgotten corners
I remember the places I have read about -
as though I really went there
How do you miss something you never touched?

        i am sick, the clouds are moving south
        i have been sick for days.
        why is there a spider on the wall?
        the sickness has stitched into my skin.
        i cannot hear the sun.

I ran from the spider until i realized she was my friend
Weaving a blanket to warm me up again
It's cold here on an island of one
I drink all the wrong medicines and wonder what's wrong

        somber diagrams of days picking bushels of thorns
        i am sick. i am well.
        the spider never tries to trap me in its web,
        there are three rocks in river
        and i have never made out to feel their wisdom.

You'll lose me on the streets of heaven
Where my hands were bound with a broken rib
But find me in the riverbed
Woven in words and spiderwebs.

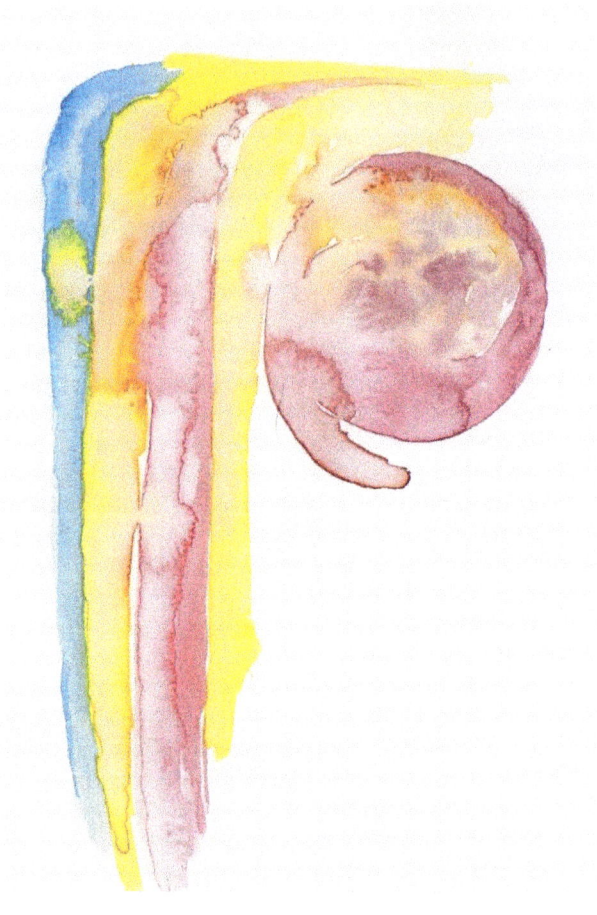

INSPIRATION COMES IN THE FROM OF SAYING NO THEN GOING ANWAY THEN REALIZING THE NO MIGHT HAVE BEEN RIGHT BUT THE YES LED TO A NIGHT THAT FIT LIKE A GLOVE

yet our inspiration was the whole mess of the night
     turning down dead-end streets
     to escape cars that looked like cops
     turning up the radio to our favorite
     Under Oath song
     turning thrifted book pages without tearing the annotated
margins dead-end
a spindle of yarn clacked around the back floorboard
collecting red clay

there, with a thick southern stinger woven into your diction,

               you sat

alone atop a pile of carefully cut chrysanthemum
counting petals and dreams that met grisly ends
counting confetti windchimes that sang of impending storms
counting faded recipe cards and recipes for disaster
bluebirds don't sing when they hear me coming anymore

there, with a homemade mud pie, we sat

with leaving present, doling out promises not to break the pearls
in the mud
     to go was the gospel our pastor
     refused to proclaim
     to go puddles around our feet while you
     stare at my world
     to go echoes and echoes and echoes

until there is only vibrations

there, with briar wisdom,
you stand with an outreached heart to say and

it turns out that the glittering castles we climbed towards were just
sparkling fog that evaporated in the desert
cracking the hard earth with splitting scars
cracking the rib cage that protects my spirit
cracking string beans over an old tub on a porch

there, with scarred hands and scarred brain folds,
you rang a bell calling us home

where the foundations of burnt bridges and shiny coins lost in
rebaptisms awaited
and still we stood in the stagnant night, breathless,
waiting
and still the fields of the west coast haunt every place you
have been
and still the fields held in my empty hand taunt the
broken record pieces in our pocket

there, by our flat tire, we understood eternity was just a phase and
that, too, would end.

It took many thousands of years for the Colorado River to dig the Grand Canyon.

SHOUTING ONLY CONFIRMS THAT THE LOUD VOICE IS TOO INSECURE TO PROCESS THE IMAGE LOOKING BACK AT THEM IN THE VANITY MIRROR

The louder you shout
The more certain I am that you fear
You would crumble in an introspective space
Medusa shattered souls in silence

     Oh, do what you do
     but know this lock works from the outside, too
     Do what you do
     but the vinegar in my silence will eat your eyes
     Oh, do what you do
     but your baritone fear will be sounding brass
     Do what you do,

27

but watch me pack my favorite shoes when I am through

I poured myself into fifty chalices
Only to be consumed and dropped to the ground
Gathering the broken pieces I see
Kings who break their toys are given kingdoms

A hummingbird flew off into the wind until thimble-sized today
It did not care about your shout, did not care about your fear
It only felt the wind and the sun and the urge to leave

Has it flown fifty times before?
Have fifty feathers fallen on frozen lakes like into a strange
chalice?

> I still hear your shout
> but only laugh now

The sound rumbling
    My maw open to drink your words
        into the dark where they will rot in this silence

The reverberation cracks the ground under your feet until you
walk on eggshells cast aside by bloodied doves
    You did not stop them from flying
    Their feathers will bury you in soft quiet

I lock the door as the doves fly toward the empty field,
        a lifeless idol is nothing
        more than an empty man.

> Hold out your tongue, let the blood fall like hot coals
> The Seraphim are not impressed, neither is your god.

Shout all that you want
The hummingbirds carry your chaos into the wind
The dove's wings will be clean again

... THEN YOU REALIZED A MILLION UNIVERSES SAT ON MY TONGUE

Cut me down and use me up
But my roots cannot be unearthed
Tethered deep in Tennessee rock
Watered by creek floods.

I contain multitudes.

Co(s)mic dynamo –
my roots wrap around sugar-sweet summers-
Sometimes, the coming gorge
smothers the child in me.

An oak that grows in shadows
is still an oak:
it has taken many seasons
to sift through the rubble
to unearth the child in me.

Disjoined jungle gym giggles echo in the hall-
I contain multitudes
anecdotally scaring my face
to feel the morning's morphine in my tissues

I contradict myself

When I catch my reflection in starlit windows
is that a lost soul?
Or a mountain lion?
They disappear into the night like

lightning bugs in June: a contradiction.

I contain multitudes.

Ragweed juxtaposition against the winter field
where the tree vibrations still

My soul burns.

There has to be salvation in stealing cars
from the junkyard –
mechanical messiah in a secular rage.

I'll be the getaway driver
speeding through midnight city lights
collecting wanderers whose rage I recognize
heading for the pine-covered hills.

We will reckon with our roots
and bathe our scars in the creek water

while the collected correspondence
between the soil
and me
waits until the bark;
trembling quiets the noise

leaving the divided-down passion to rest
I contain multitudes as
my soul burns.

SO, I STOPPED

breathe in-
let grief sit like a companion, not an accuser

breathe out-
obliterate the way one describes blue

breathe in-
shatter oligarchs of relevance

breathe out-
embrace stillness inside the liturgy of breath.

Rid your lungs of the poison
that floats down from the capitalistic castle
Shed the skin that was once soft, now scarred
Climb from the cocoon, you carefully wove from realization
Burn the path that was trampled by clinging boas-
no one can pass without
                              Breathing in

nirodhaksana in the river that runs from mountain to heart

breathe in-
i am, i am not, i will be

breathe out-
let the flood run into the obsidian gulf

breathe in-
the razor blades of anxiety are part of being human

31

breathe out-
to doubt is divine

I grip at my gasping lungs -
Do the branches of reading trees make enough
oxygen for me to live off of?
Book banning deprives me of what it takes to live
I grieve the humanity obliterated by floods of authority

       nature breathes in without our permission-

breathe in-
the creek awaits

breathe out-
when will i be free enough to go?

Eventually
     The River will rust these chains.

33

AND I TOOK A BREATH

the grey clouds are back today,
     hills and hills of colorless nature
     stretch over the mountains.
they do not come with rain, nor thunder,
as though they willfully exist without being heard
the moths do not fly today
      paintbrushes lay strewn at my feet beneath thorns
fog creeps in - tumbling slowly like memories
do I lay here or do I seek the trees

the corner of this room held the dark longer,
      today mounds and mounds of daytime come to life,
at least silence holds back the morning
until i am forced to move out of the shadows
i wonder if the light will burn my tired skin
if i can find the will to shuffle through the puzzle pieces
pull out the will to emerge
snap it into place - it's just one piece, but it is enough
the frameless borrowed photographs have eyes
      they look at me, i should goat them down,
they look at me
why am observed by this floor
can it lie and tell me it is possible to fall into the dark
i lay down in the hills
beneath the thorns and the eyes
eventually
        the clouds   will float
                away

they always do

april is for lovers but here it is february and i am falling in love
with every tarnished leaf and stained shirt i see, come with me,
we will go down swinging with passion as barbwire and art as a
grave- dead she said, then looked at a ripped canvas and said life

the record hangs on the wall like a daguerreotype
            bleeding lost catacomb youth
with carbon-14 worth
dead she said, art is dead when it no longer bleeds

unearth the golden coffin and open it
let out the prisms of light buried by
one too many roses with thorns
cut the wires and leave them for the spiders
can you resurrect what no longer bleeds

                    i bleed,
                    i bleed,
                    i am bleeding

will this be art
                when
                        when
what if there is not another   when?

is my art dead if i never bring it to life?

i plant a cemetery of poems that never made it to the page

sometimes I mourn for them -
i scribble words and sketches on paper bags
and receipts in their honor

what if there is not another when?

dead she said, as she poured kerosene onto my canvas.

will we ever really fade if art is what we leave behind?
burn it down, then - all crackling canvases and canary cries
i don't want to stick around –
     i'd bleed out
when art crumbles and dies

  dead she said, as she flipped over the table and
       walked into the yellow fog night
       wearing a familiar grin.

www.ingramcontent.com/pod-product-compliance
Lightning Source LLC
Chambersburg PA
CBHW051249120626
46547CB00014B/1861

* 9 7 8 1 9 6 7 2 3 0 0 2 0 *